Visit us at

GritUpSeries.com

AMKCounseling.com

ISBN 978-0-9890102-1-4

Lorem ipsum
Special thanks to the brain squad KH, KK & MV

Emotion

Commotion

CONFUSED

ANGER

GOOFY

ANNOYED

BORED

GUILT

EXCITEMENT

SADNESS

JOYFUL

HAPPINESS

RELAXED

HOPEFUL

EMBARASSED

WORRIED

LONELY

ENERGETIC

Helping children calm their intense emotions

Written by Abbie Kelley, MA, LCPC

Illustrated by Mary Kelley

Hi Mandy, what are you doing?

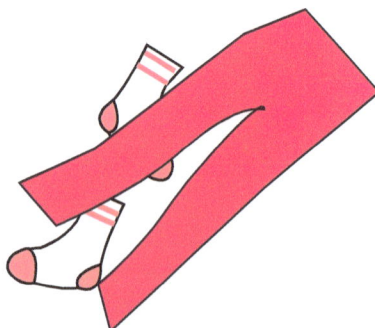

I'm thinking about my
friend's sleepover party!
I'm so excited!

It's a
PARTY!

2

Aren't you supposed to
be cleaning your room?

Oh my gosh, it's a sleepover party! I can't stop thinking about all the fun we are going to have!

3

You are supposed to be cleaning your room but...

goodies

FuN

you are too distracted
thinking about the party!

PiZZA

FRiENDS

MUSiC

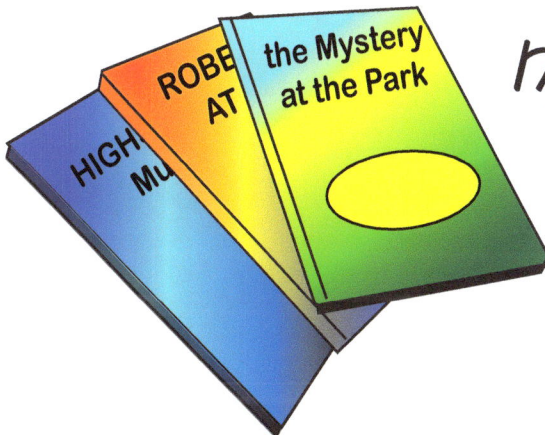

MOVieS

It seems like the excitement is causing
a commotion inside your body.

GAMES!

MUSIC!

FRIENDS!

POPCORN!

PIZZA!

SLEEPOVER!

You can not hear me... excitement has taken over your body.

Getting Gritty: Think about a time when excitement took over your body and what happened.

8

When emotions take over our body
we call it **emotion commotion**.

It's happening to you because
you feel super excited, but this can
happen with any emotion.

Getting Gritty: Can you identify the different emotions Mandy is feeling?

When **emotion commotion** happens
we are no longer in charge
and often make poor choices.

Like how you are choosing
not to clean your room.

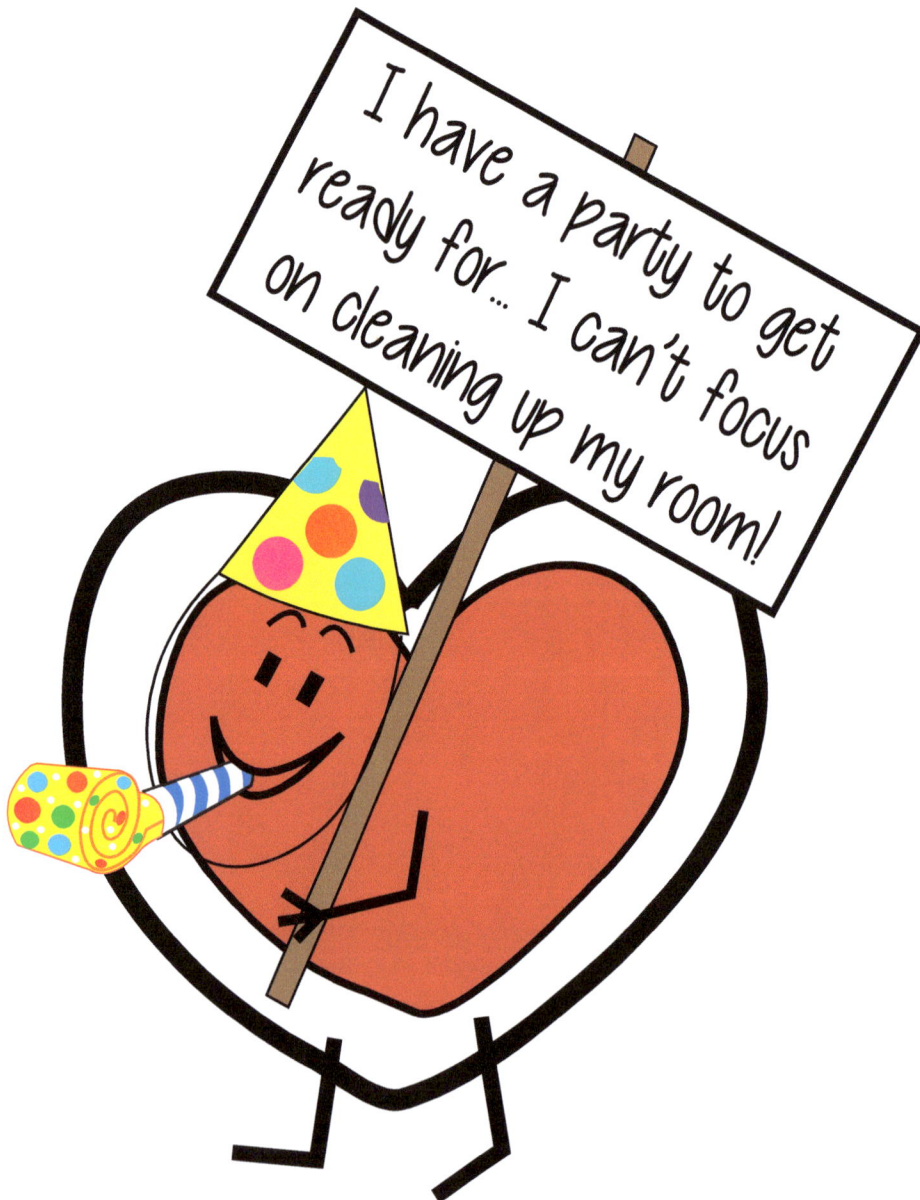

The problem is, once the emotions calm down, you are left to clean up after them!

"What do you mean by "clean up after them?"

If excitement takes over and prevents you from cleaning your room, you won't be able to go to the party, right?

Oh that CANNOT happen! I need to go!

Getting Gritty: If anger took over your body, what might be some consequences?

It's happened to you before, remember?

Ugh, you mean when I hit my brother and couldn't go to Mallory's house?

Exactly.

14

It's important to listen to your emotions.
They create reactions in your body.
We've seen this with you already...

My thoughts were racing fast...

pizza, friends, games,
fun, movies, music, goodies...

I wasn't able to
listen to you...

I was really
distracted...

The stronger the emotion, the larger the reaction. There are different reactions for different emotions.

Super Excited →

Body wants to move
Not listening
Acting too silly
Not doing what you're
supposed to do

Really Mad →

Yelling
Body feels hot
Saying hurtful words
Not doing what you're
supposed to do

Super Sad →

Crying
Can't focus
Body feels heavier
Not interested in
activities

Getting Gritty: What happens to your body when these emotions take over?

16

Emotions help us make good choices.
They can be very helpful,
but not when they cause a commotion!

I feel happy when I hang
out with my friends.

But, sometimes I feel nervous
when I have to take a test.

How do I stop emotion commotion?

First you have to recognize the signs
of **emotion commotion** in your body.

Sometimes it feels like there are

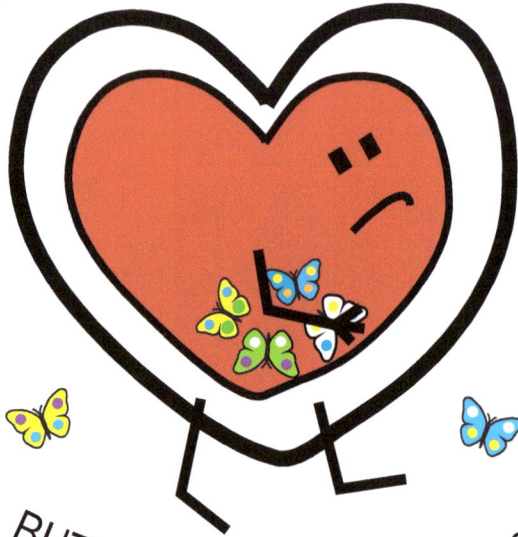

BUTTERFLIES in my stomach...

and other times I feel like WASPS

are buzzing around in there.

How were you feeling about the party?

Oh my gosh, I was so excited!

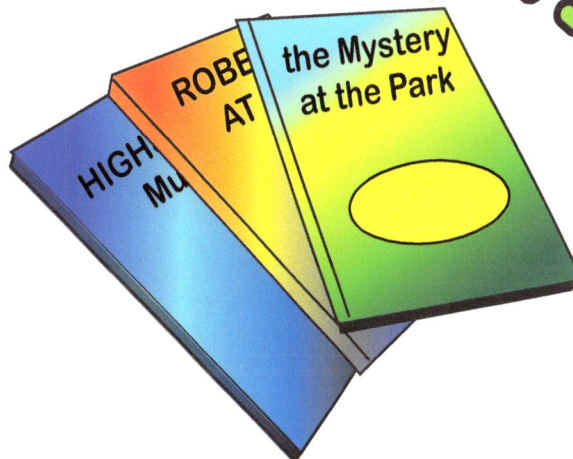

What were you doing?

I was talking fast. I was playing with my basketball. I wasn't really listening and I wasn't cleaning my room. I guess my emotions were causing a commotion.

Yes, and your body reacted in lots of different ways.

Your thoughts started racing real fast.

pizza, friends, games, fun, movie, music...

You were daydreaming.

Your cheeks were getting hot.

You couldn't focus on what you were supposed to be doing.

Your heart was beating faster.

You were unable to sit still.

You weren't able to listen to anyone else.

Once you recognize your emotions taking over, you can take steps to help calm down.

exercise

deep breathing

Take a bath.

count

distract yourself

Listen to music.

Getting Gritty: Name three things you can do to calm down at home, school and away from home.

talk to a friend
or family member

Stretching

relax your muscles

Try drawing or doodling.

guided
meditation

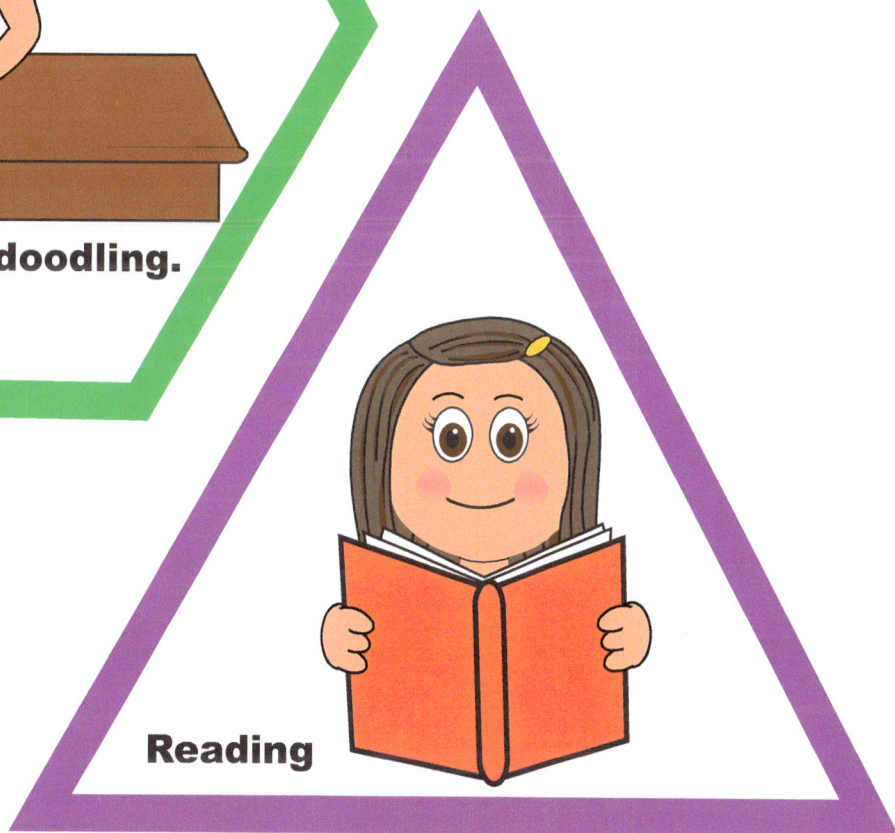

Reading

Breathing is a great way to calm down. Try to take a deep breath in through your nose for three seconds

then breathe out through your mouth for 3 seconds.

Repeat this.

You can also stretch or move your body.

I feel calmer now and my emotions feel less intense.

Getting Gritty: What are some new calming skills you can try?

So Mandy, now that you are calmer, can you expain to me what **emotion commotion** is?

27

Emotion commotion is what happens when emotions take over your body. When this happens you have to stop and calm down so you can make good choices.

That was a great explanation Mandy!

At times you may have a difficult time saying or understanding what you are feeling. Hang in there, work to identify your emotions when you are feeling them or even after they're gone. The more you are able to identify your emotions the better you will be at preventing **emotion commotion**.

Self-awareness is the ability to accurately recognize your feelings and understand how they affect your behaviors.

Self-management allows you to develop the ability to manage your emotions and control your behaviors. This can be very empowering! Keep practicing and ask adults for help when you need it. You can also ask adults or family members about their emotions. The more others discuss their emotions, the more you will learn about your own!

www.ingramcontent.com/pod-product-compliance
Lightning Source LLC
Chambersburg PA
CBHW040022050426
42452CB00002B/88